Bob and Larry's ABC's

by Phil Vischer

Thomas Nelson, Inc.
Nashville

Art Direction:
Ron Eddy

Lead 3D Illustrator:
Aaron Hartline

3D Illustrators:
Thomas Danen, Robert Ellis,
Mike Laubach, Joe McFadden,
Joe Sapulich and Nathan Tungseth

Render Management:
Jennifer Combs and Ken Greene

Copyright © 1997
by Big Idea Productions

Illustrations Copyright © 1997
by Big Idea Productions

Published in Nashville, Tennessee, by Tommy Nelson™,
a division of Thomas Nelson, Inc.

Library of Congress Cataloging-in-Publication Data
Vischer, Phil.
    Bob and Larry's ABC's / by Phil Vischer.
        p. cm.
    Summary: Bob the Tomato and Larry the Cucumber teach the
letters of the alphabet using common objects and simple rhymes.
    ISBN 0-8499-1508-2
    1. English language — Alphabet — Juvenile literature.
[1. Alphabet.] I. Title.
PE1155.V57 1997
428.1 — dc21
    [E]   97-34567
                                                    CIP
                                                    AC

Printed in the United States of America

98 99 00 01 02 03 BVG 9 8 7 6 5 4 3

Dear Parent

We believe that children are a
gift from God and that helping
them learn and grow is nothing less
than a divine privilege.

With that in mind, we hope these
"Veggiecational" books provide years
of rocking chair fun as they teach
your kids fundamental concepts
about the world God made.

– Phil Vischer

President
Big Idea Productions

If learning your letters is part of your job,
Meet Alphabet Larry
and Alphabet Bob!

A is for Archibald.
    Look at his coat!

B is for **B**ob and his
big bamboo boat!

C is for cucumber
(this one's called Larry).
It's also for carrots with
chocolate to carry!

**D** is for **d**octor and **d**oorway and **D**ad.

E is for **e**ngine that makes Pa Grape sad!

F is for flowers from Flibber-o-loo . . .

G is for George
and for
Grandma Grape, too!

H is for **hairbrush**. Oh, where could it be?

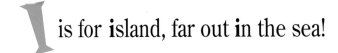

I is for **i**sland, far out **in** the sea!

J is for Junior! And Jimmy and Jerry …
The very best buddies of Bobby & Larry!

K is for **k**ettle and **k**ing,
and you'll find
It also reminds us
to always be **k**ind.

L is for Laura ...

and M is for Mom.
She's **m**aking some **m**uffins
with Junior and Tom!

N is for **n**ecktie and

Nebby K. Nezzer ...

O is for ocean that hides sunken treasure!

P is for penguins and popular peas …
A hero with plungers and singing palm trees!

Q is for **Q**werty, who
tells us the truth.

R is for **R**osie and dear old Aunt **R**uth!

S is for shepherd with **s**ix **s**illy **s**heep
That need **s**tanding up
    when they fall in a heap!

T is for **t**oy box and bright, red **t**omato

U is for **u**nderwear
on a potato?

"**V** is for **veggies**!" says Alphabet Larry.
"We grow in the forest,
we grow on the prairie!

Wherever you find us,
in sand or in sod,
Remember we all were
made special by God!"

"But not just us veggies, as **W** knows,
God made the **w**hole **w**orld!
That's **w**hy everyone grows!"

Here is the end of the alphabet. See?
Just three little letters left ...

X, Y and Z!

"We need those three letters,"
says Larry, " to say ...
X-ray the yellow
zucchini today!"

Alphabet Larry and Alphabet Bob!
It's time to go home now ...
        you've finished your job!

Go back to your rooms;
        feed your fish and your cats.
But please, first take off those ridiculous hats!